WHAT[illegible]ER MAGIC YOU NEED

WHATEVER MAGIC YOU NEED

Scott Andrew James

Speedy Race Press

ISBN: 978-0-9858434-1-0

Layout and design by Liya James

Speedy Race Press
a division of Giant Panda Studio
4600 Mueller Blvd. #2059 Austin, TX 78723

www.scottandrewjames.com

For Liya, Kaili and Hamms.
You make my heart sing :)

And for Jeanie.
Thank you for believing.

And for you, dear reader.
May you find whatever magic you need.

When I began typing poems, it was a way to dig myself out of what felt like a deep, suffocating hole. I gave myself a mission to write and give away a thousand poems in a year. I took requests, gave poems as gifts, and generally set about putting words to the magic we all share. Completing that mission changed my life, and I have never looked back.

I've now written and given away thousands more poems, and it feels good to put a voice to that light. Most poems I type on the spot and give away, never seeing them again. I believe each has its own journey and ripple effect in this world, and it is a blessing to be part of that flow.

The poems in this book I have held onto because they have held on to me. I give them to you now, along with whatever magic they carry.

May you find your way out of every darkness, and move always further into the light.

Scott Andrew James
August 2019

clarity

i am not
who i thought
i was

and for that
i am
forever
grateful

The only beginning
that matters

is the one
happening

right now.

we are only
as far away
from each other

as the space
we do not reach
across.

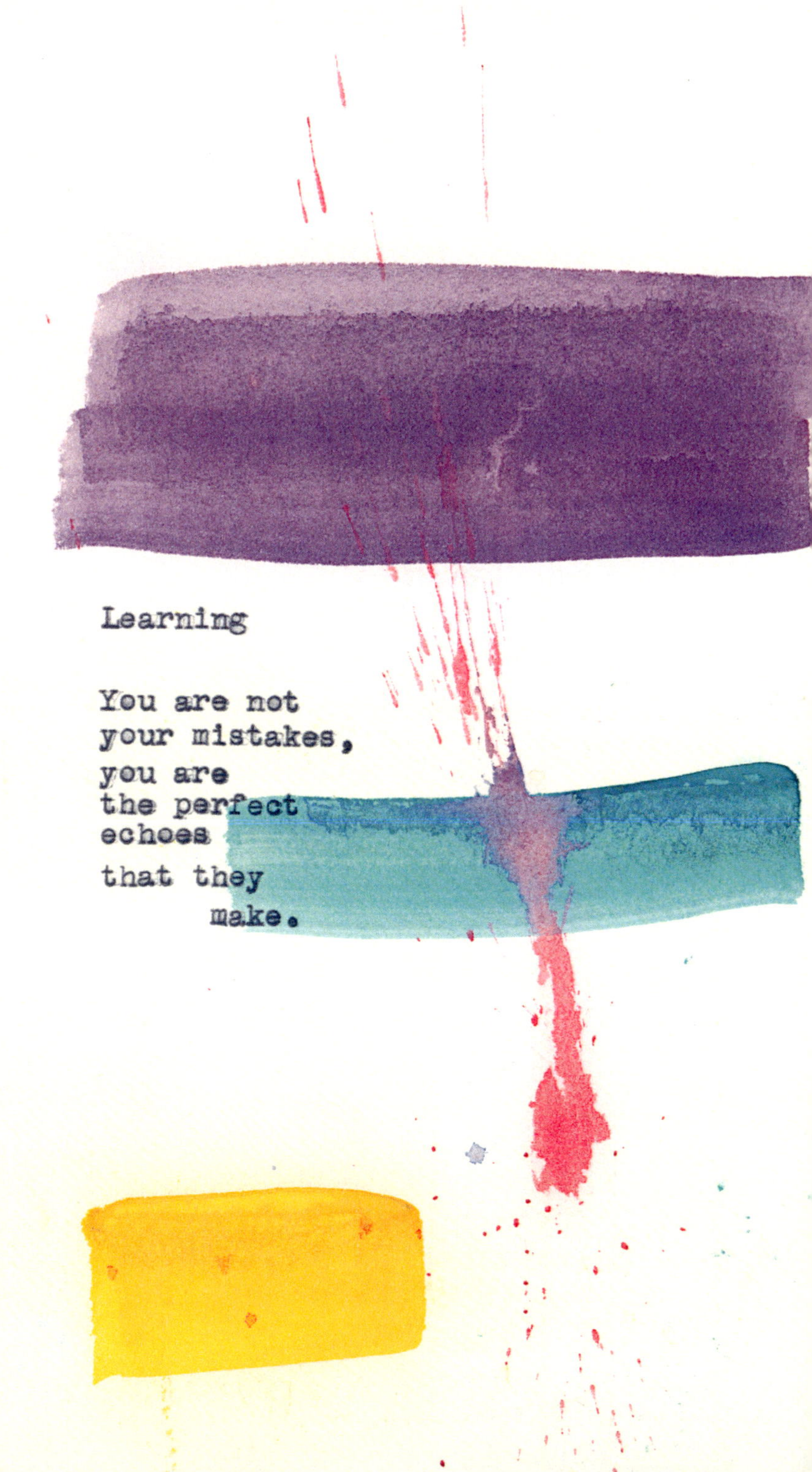

Learning

You are not
your mistakes,
you are
the perfect
echoes
that they
make.

Pavement

Believe,

and the road
appears.

Not because
of some magic,

but because
you are walking
and you can see it.

Let us dance
with the possible

and make instruments
of the mistakes
playing alongside
the truth now
in tune.

Next

Oh, flower --
crouching underneath
this fallen leaf,
blooming anyway
& with irreverant joy.

You remind me
that I am right
where I need to be.

Awareness

What do you want
from the day
that is not already
exploding like
a thousand spring

b l o s s o m s

in slow motion

just
for
you?

To be seen is
one thing.
A hard thing, but
just one
thing.

To be seen for
who we are is
even harder.

It means
we must know
and be brave enough
to show it.

Advice

My cousin writes,
asking for advice.

Do I tell her
what I would do if I were
her? What I would do if it were me?
What I think she should absolutely
definitely not do?

Do I ramble on & on about goals and
possibilities? Choices &
consequences? Sending a message vs.
turning the other cheek?

Do I sit quietly maybe say to follow
her heart, tell her it will
work itself out? Be the change
you want to see, etc?

No. I do none of these things.

I look out the window, turn off
my computer and start to write
a letter that will say something
in words,

but really just mean
I love you.

Nice Job, Rain

The rain is doing
whatever it wants,
totally
out of control,

it's in my hair,
my eyes, & my shoes!

I just saw some rain
turn into a stream
and hightail it
down the gutter.

I tried
to reason with
a puddle,
Like,
why don't
you do this
when we're sleeping?
No dice.

It just kept
falling, running,
and gathering
up with other
raindrops.

Ok. Truth is,
I'm jealous.

Nice job, rain.
Keep it up :)

I was the answer
then
I was the problem
then
I was the answer again.

Have you ever
been in love?

Belief

Welcome back,
belief --

it has been
hard to know
what I was doing
without you.

it's like dancing
without a floor
and forgetting
I have wings.

Birthday

One day
is not enough
to be born,

The first one
is free.

The rest?

Your heart
needs to do
the pushing.

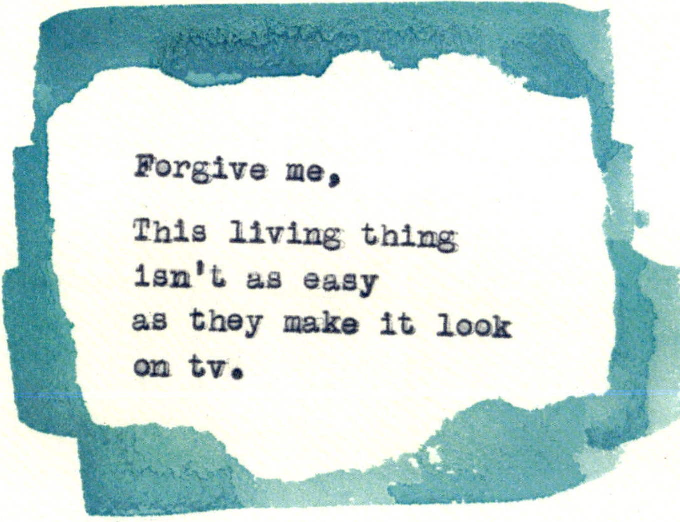
Forgive me,
This living thing
isn't as easy
as they make it look
on tv.

Bamboo Blues

We planted
the bamboo as if
it would just grow,

but

it turns out
it needs love & water
just like
us.

home is not
so much a place
as a moment,

that feeling when
everything
is where it should be.

Even you.

Oh, weekend...

Why do your
Sunday nights
never seem to keep
your Saturday
morning promises?

How many times
do we hear
what is said
but not
what is meant?

Oh,
how the truth
robs us
of our certainty

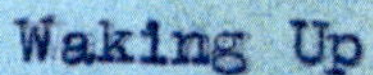

Waking Up

When you wake up
and open your eyes

are you willing
to see
what you're looking at?

The answer
is a secret
you have
to tell
yourself.

Rhythm Apart

We have nothing to sing
but what's in our hearts.

Don't let the world
tear your rhythm apart.

Now off I go
with this
ragged question mark

tucked into
my back pocket

holding
all the truth
I'll ever need.

What Next?

Do what makes
your soul smile.

Then,
keep going.

Photo Credit: Dylan John Western

About the Author

Scott Andrew James is a poet who believes in everyday magic. His work explores the nature of transformation and the healing power of creativity. He performs watercolor & typewriter poetry across the country, taking requests to create poems in the moment. He lives in Austin, Texas with his wife, daughter, and their pug.

For more about his work, visit: ScottAndrewJames.com

Made in the USA
San Bernardino, CA
05 September 2019